NESTING PYRAMIDS

This curious mathematical model consists of six linked pyramids which will fold inwards to make a cube and also outwards to create a rhombic dodecahedron. This is a polyhedron with twelve faces, each of them a rhombus.
For more information see pages 2 & 3 of the minibook.

The other pieces for this model are on page 3.

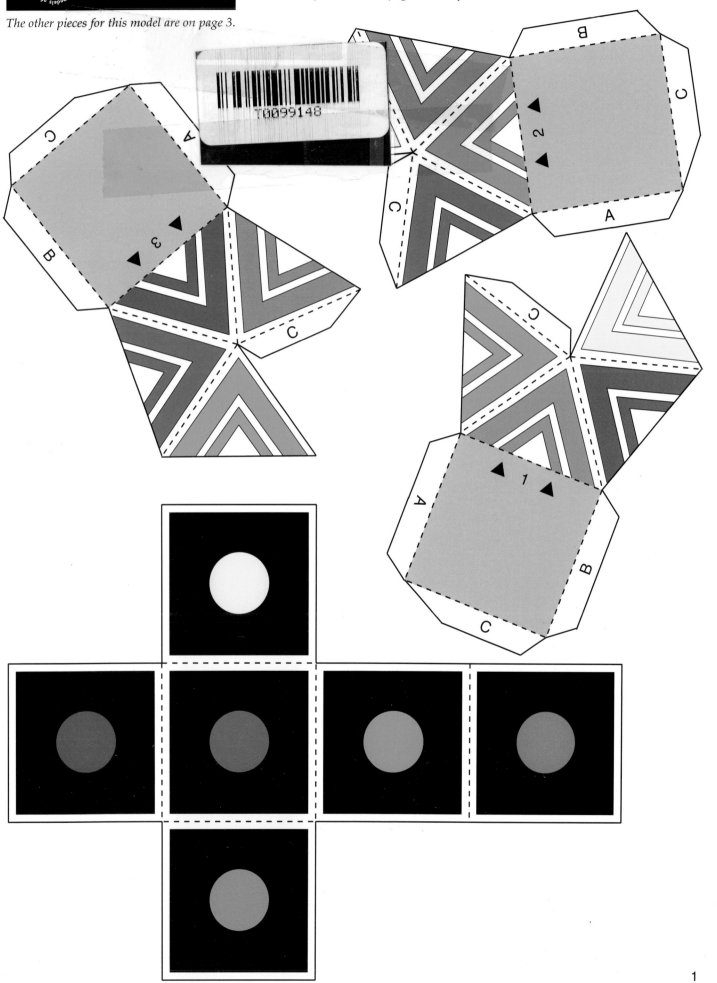

NESTING
PYRAMIDS

B

C

C

A

A

C

C

A

B

B

C

C

▼ 3 ▼

▶ 6 ▶   ▶ 5 ▶   ▶ 1 ▶ ◀ 2 ◀
▶   ▶   ▶   ◀

▲ 4 ▲

NESTING PYRAMIDS

The other pieces for this model are on page 1.

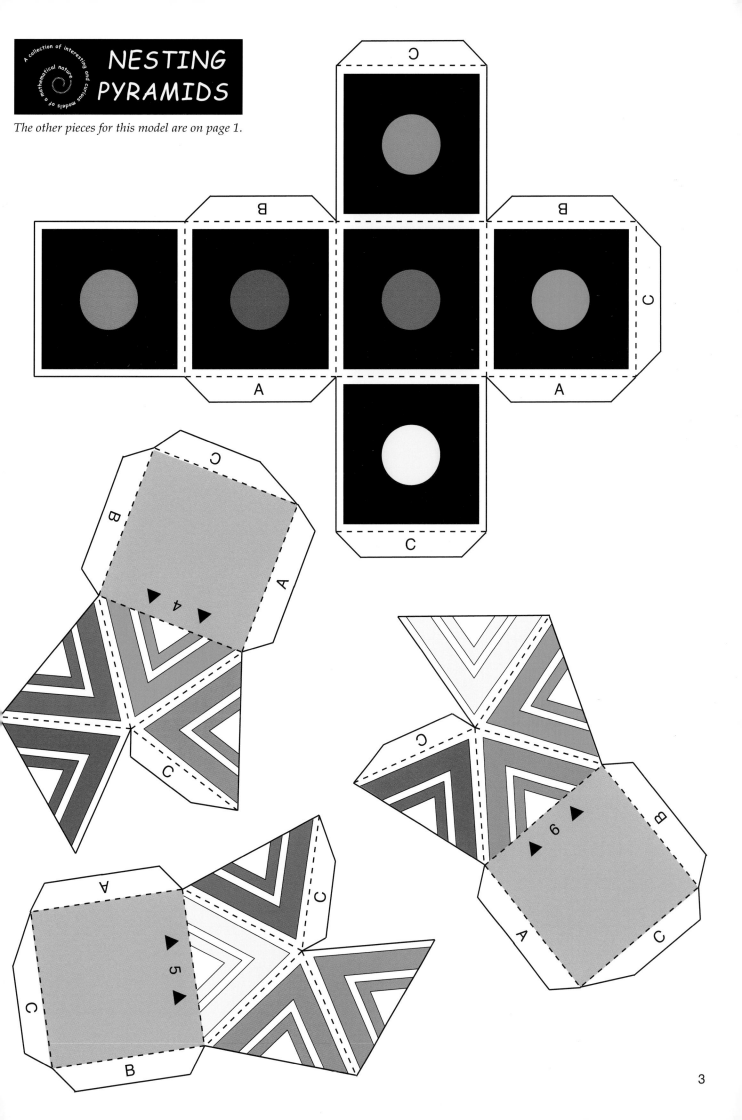

B   B

C

C

C

A   A

C

C

B

B

A

A

C   C

A

C

C

B

This curious model is made from six tetrahedra in the form of a ring and will rotate endlessly through its centre, forming a regular hexagonal outline at two stages of the rotation. The stars and their coloured backgrounds give a preview of which colours are about to appear. For more information, see page 4 of the minibook.

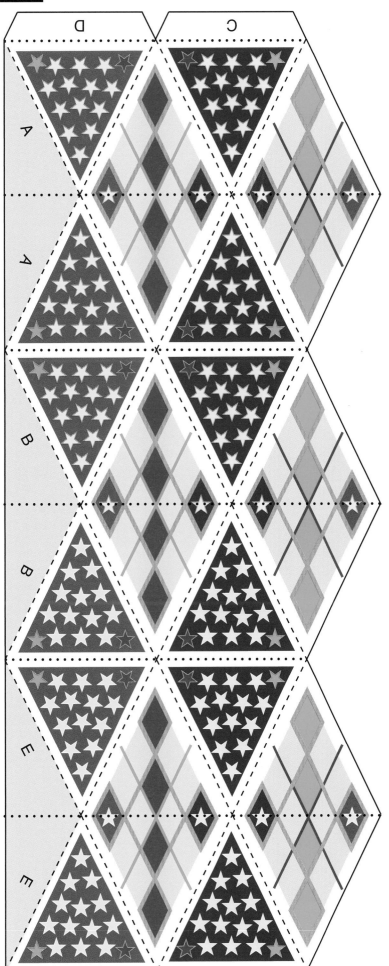

A

A

B

B

E

E

C

D

THE RAINBOW FLOWER

These two rainbow coloured pieces glue together to make a model with very curious properties. It will bloom and grow like a flower and the colours burst surprisingly out of a black interior. For more information, see page 5 of the minibook.

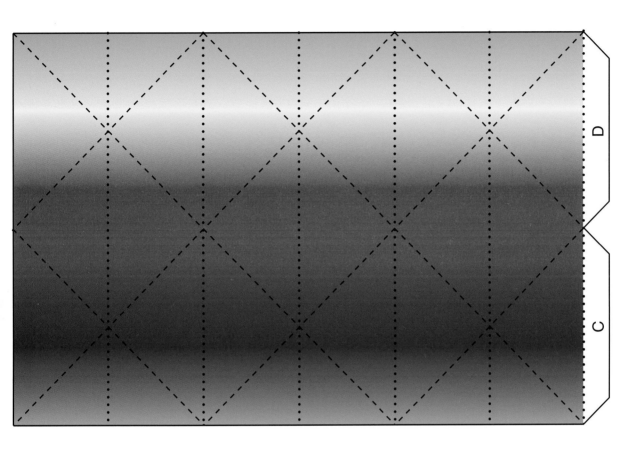

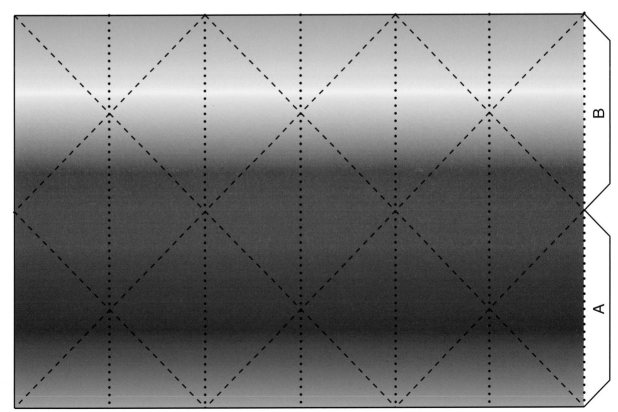

THE RAINBOW
FLOWER

B

A

D

C

VANISHING AREA

The three pieces of this curious model fit into the same tray in two different ways, one of which seems to leave a red hole with an area of about one square centimetre. The other way leaves no space at all. How can this be and where does this area go to or come from? For more information, see pages 6 & 7 of the minibook.

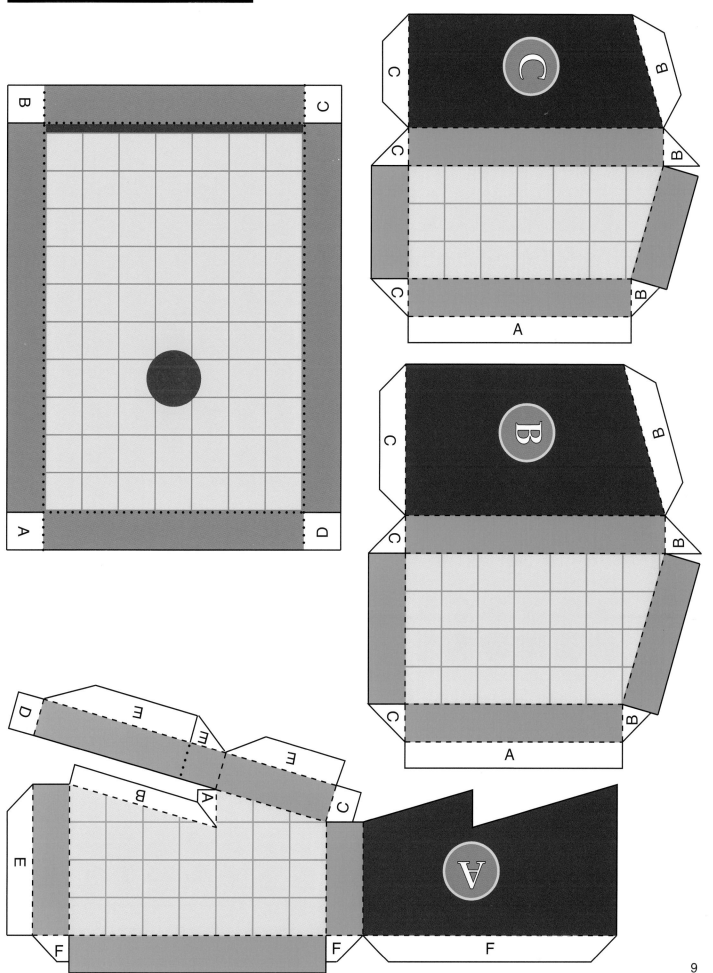

A

B

C

B

B

C

B

C

B

A

D A

B

C

B

A

B

C D

E

E E

C

E

F F F

SHAPES OF CONSTANT WIDTH

This collection of models demonstrates a very curious fact, namely that there are other shapes besides a circle which are of constant width. Roll them along the channel and see how apparently 'lumpy' shapes will none the less roll smoothly and reach to a constant height. For more information, see pages 8 & 9 of the minibook.

The other pieces of this collection are on page 13.

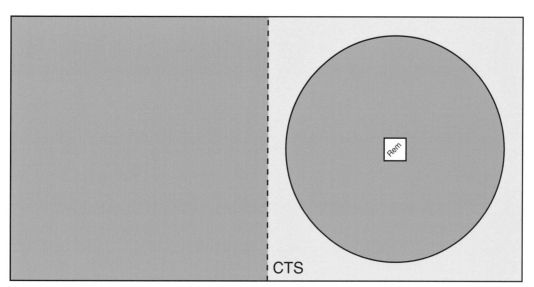

This shape and the similar pieces on page 13 are first glued to their handles using numbers 1 to 4, then glued back to back matching the ▲s and the numbers 5 to 8. The final shape is then cut out looking at the side marked CTS meaning Cut This Side.

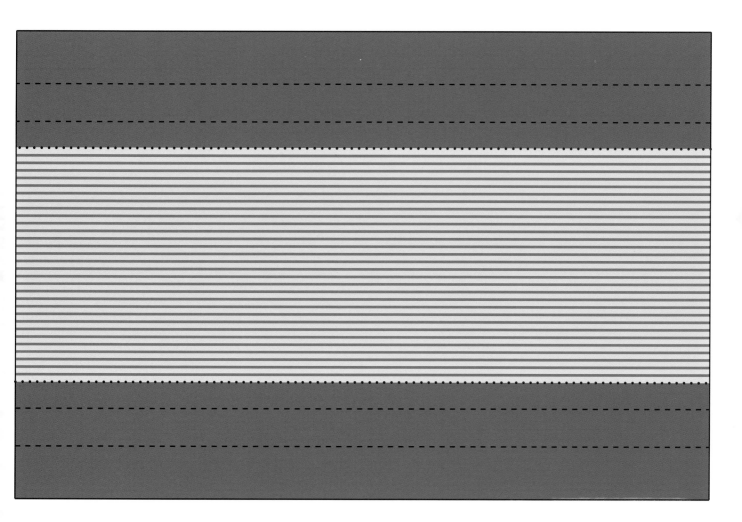

SHAPES OF
CONSTANT WIDTH

5   5

    1
5   1 1   5 5   ◀ ▲ ▶   5
    1   ▼

5   5

B   B   B

B   B   B

A   A   A

A   A   A

The other pieces of this collection are on page 11.

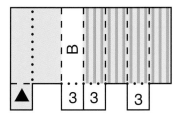

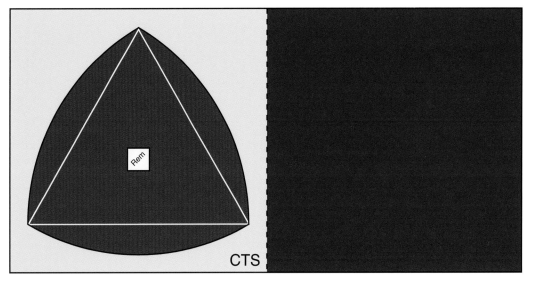

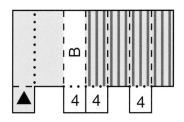

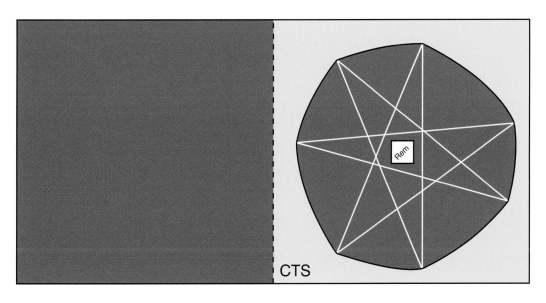

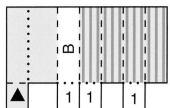

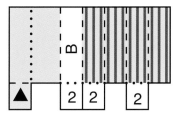

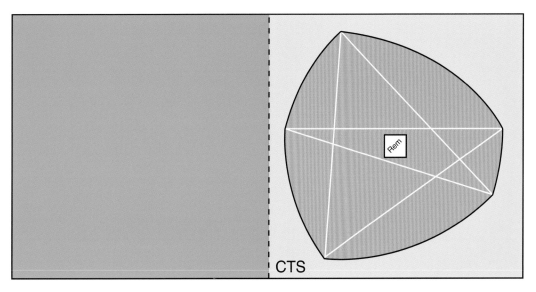

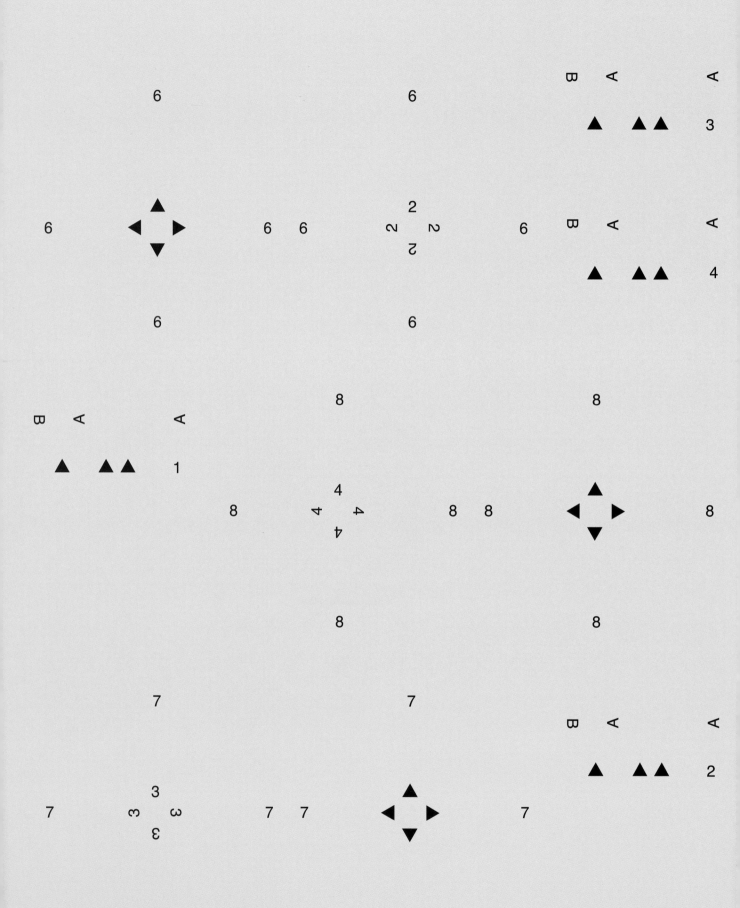

THE DOUBLE HELIX

Glue these two pieces together and create a curious double helix model. The two edges spiral separately at a constant distance apart linked by coloured 'steps'. See how it compares with the double helix of the DNA of all living creatures. For more information, see page 10 of the minibook.

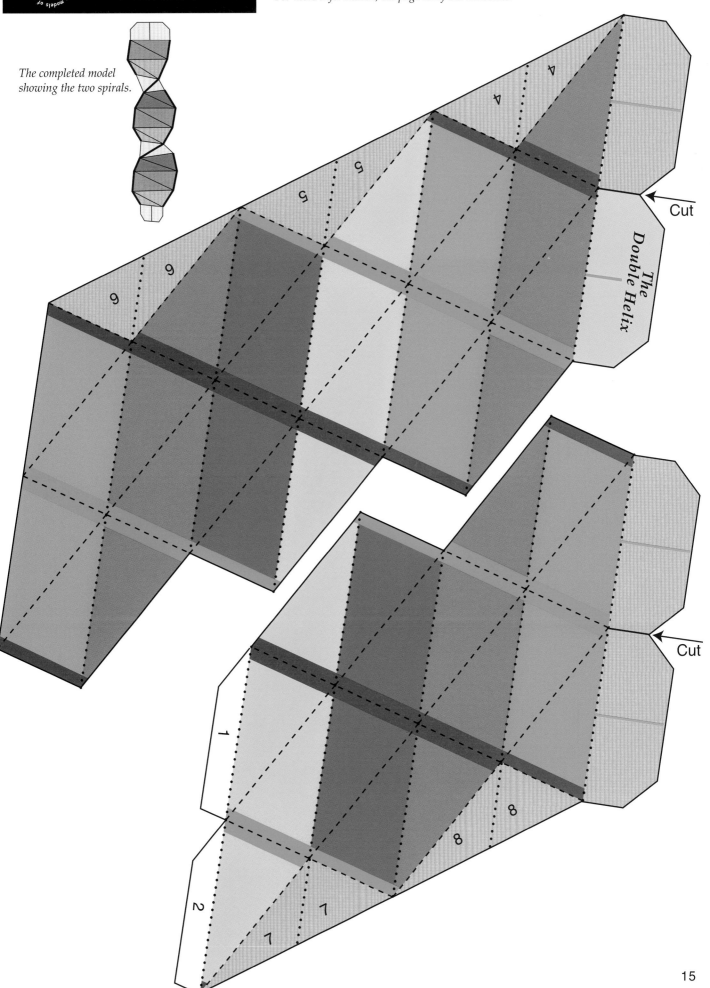

The completed model showing the two spirals.

The Double Helix

Cut

Cut

3

3

2

4

8

4

8

5

9

7

5

1

7

6

6

9

POP-UP PYRAMIDS

The two pop-up pyramids of this model are set in opposing directions, one inside the other. They are curious and intriguing in that just as they become parallel, the smaller one disappears from view. For more information about creating pop-ups, see page 11 of the minibook.

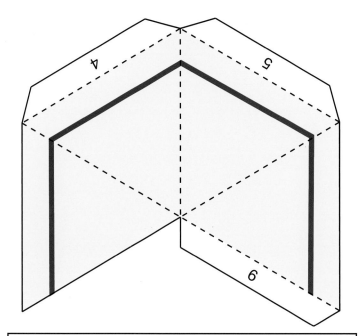

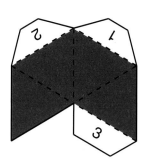

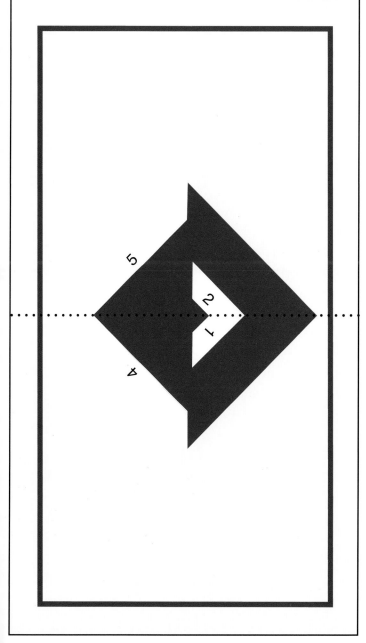

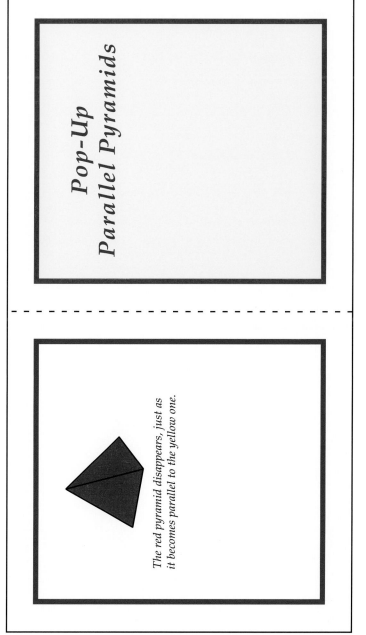

Pop-Up Parallel Pyramids

The red pyramid disappears, just as it becomes parallel to the yellow one.

DOUBLE-SIDED MAGIC SQUARE

The other pieces of this puzzle are on page 21.

This ingenious puzzle requires careful logical thinking about magic squares and the arrangements of colours on the front and back in order to come up with a solution. When you find it, then the magic squares on the upper side and the underside have a remarkable number of properties. For more information, see page 12 of the minibook. For the solution see page 15.

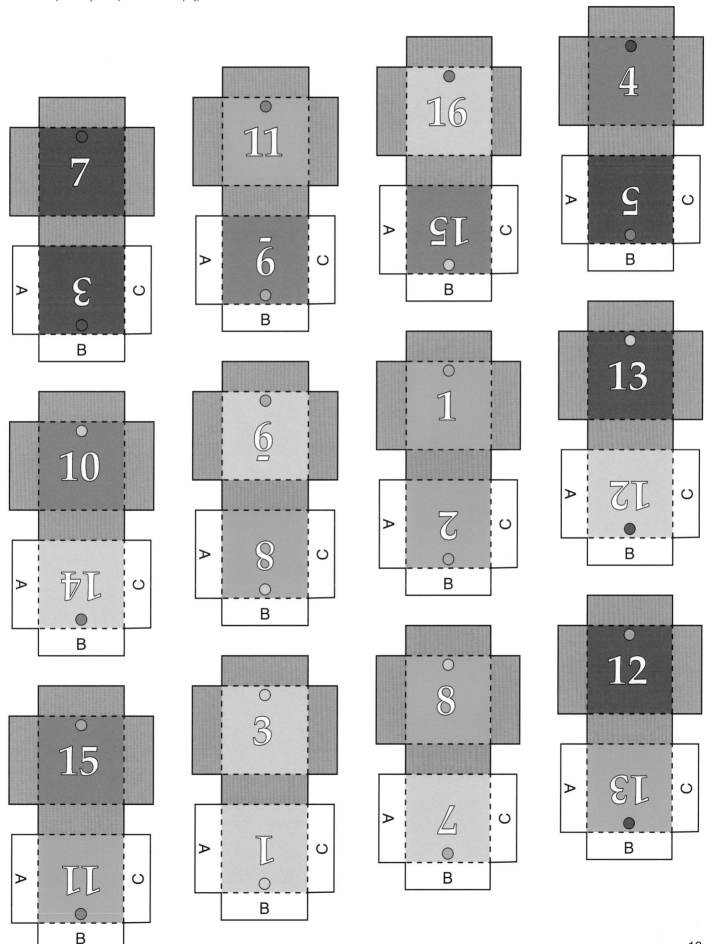

DOUBLE-SIDED
MAGIC SQUARE

B
C
A
B
B
C
A
C
B
A
C
A
B
A
A

B
B
C
A
B
C
A
B
A
C
A
C
A

B
B
C
A
B
A
C
B
C
A
A
C
A

The other pieces for this puzzle are on page 19.

E | F

Remove Remove Remove Remove

Arrange the sixteen squares so that

Remove Remove Remove Remove

all rows, columns and diagonals add up to 34

Remove Remove Remove Remove

and all 2 x 2 groups of numbers add up to 34

Remove Remove Remove Remove

Hint: On one side all the squares in a row are the same colour.
On the other side all the squares in a column are the same colour.

C | D

Remove Remove Remove Remove

Remove Remove Remove Remove

Remove Remove Remove Remove

Remove Remove Remove Remove

A | B

The Double-sided Magic Square Puzzle

▲ 2 ▲

B
C 9 A
2

B
C 4 A
5

B
C 10 A
9

B
C 16 A
14

F

E

A

C

B

A

C

▲ 2 ▲

D

▼ 1 ▼

C

B

A

C

B

A

C

B

B

A

A

C

▲ 1 ▲

B

TRIANGULAR DISSECTION

This model consists of three linked pieces which fold in two directions to demonstrate some important properties of the angles and the area of triangles. It looks very good also! For more information, see page 13 of the minibook.

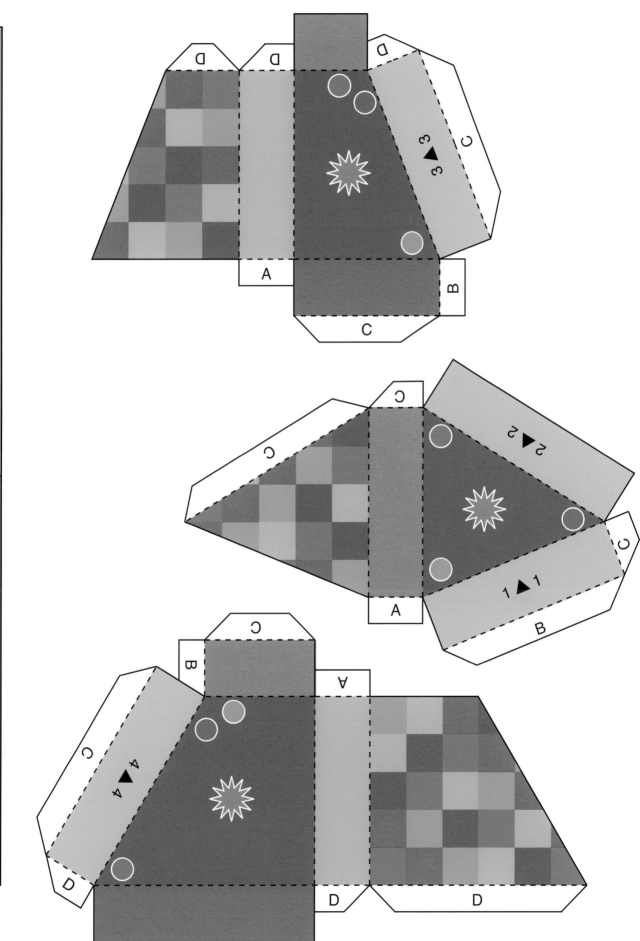

TRIANGULAR DISSECTION

D D D

4 ▲ 4

C

B

C

A

2 ▲ 2

C

C

C

B

1 ▲ 1

A

A

B

C

3 ▲ 3

C

D D D

FLIP-FLOP PARALLELEPIPEDS

The other pieces of this model are on page 27.

These three pieces glue together in an ingenious way to make a curious model with two separate holes passing through it. It also has the curious property of squashing completely flat in two different directions. All its faces are rhombuses and on page 14 of the minibook there is more information about it.

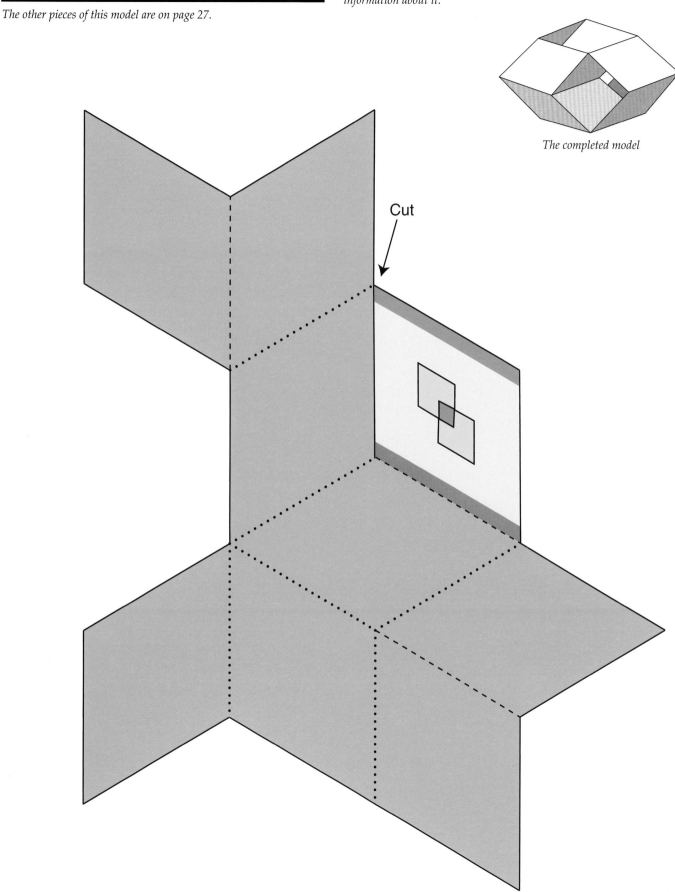

The completed model

Cut

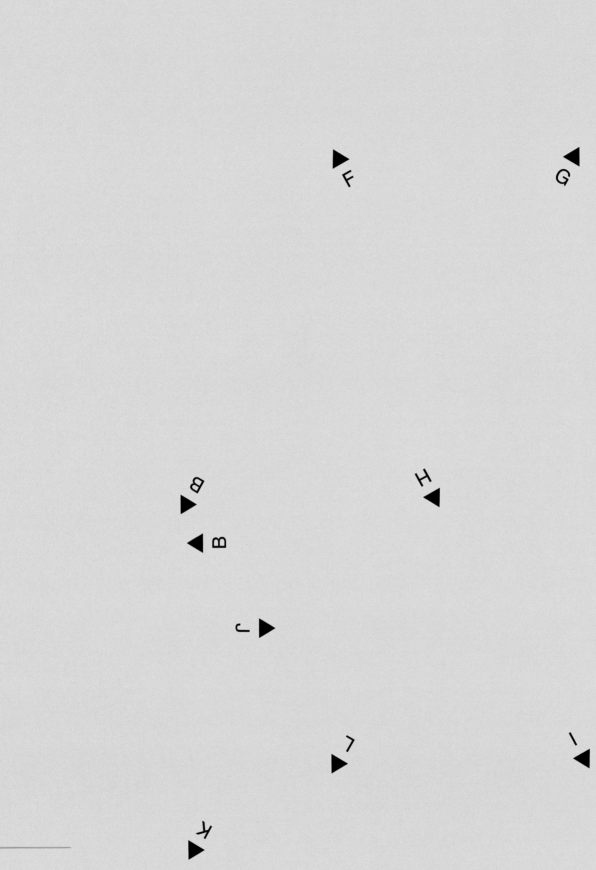

The other piece of this model is on page 25.

Cut

Cut

Score along ◄ - - - - ►
and then cut out pages 3 to 8.
Instructions for making the minibook are on the inside of the back cover.

The Rhombic Dodecahedron

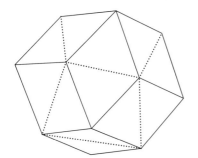

It is curious that the six pyramids which will fold together to make a cube will also fold outwards to make a rhombic dodecahedron, a polyhedron with twelve rhombic faces.

Note that four rhombuses meet at some of its vertices and three at others and that all the edges of this rhombic dodecahedron are of length m.

The void at the centre is a cube of side l and in the model it can be filled with the other ordinary cube that is provided. It is the same size but has been coloured as a mirror image. This means that when the linked pyramids are wrapped round it, the colours can be made to match.

Investigations of the rhombic dodecahedron
1. What is the formula for its volume?
2. Show that the angles of the faces are 70.52° and 109.48° (decimal degrees)
3. What is its surface area?
4. What is the diameter of its circumscribing sphere?

3

Rainbow Flower

This is a delightful and curious model and to make it bloom, hold it gently in the fingers of both hands. Gently rotate it outwards and the middle will then rise up and open out. As the rotation continues, the centre turns over and becomes the outside, only to reappear at the centre as the sequence continues without end. Who could have guessed that right-angled isosceles triangles could behave like this.

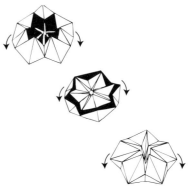

If you have difficulty in making it work, check that all the folds have in fact been folded the right way. The net is correct! However the flower will only bloom and show its amazing properties if every one of them is folded as it should be.

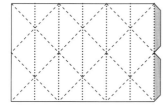

The net is given here for you to make more of these polyhedra flowers which you can decorate yourself to bring out their flower-like qualities. Draw it on plain paper, preferably a thickish cartridge. All the angles are either 45° or 90° and you need two pieces like this.

5

The Paradoxical Area Model

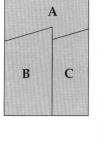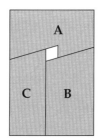

This model is an impressive one because there are only three pieces and one of them is never moved. Simply by exchanging pieces B and C, a substantial amount of area above the red spot seems to appear or vanish. The puzzle is to explain where it goes to or comes from.

After you have tried it a few times you may notice a red line along the bottom which you can see when the hole above has disappeared and which you cannot see when the hole is there. This is the explanation. The squarish rectangular area becomes distributed as a long narrow rectangle, not very much wider than a line.

When trying this paradoxical model on others, arrange the three pieces so that the sides with the squares are uppermost. Counting the squares adds to the confusion and takes the eye away from the red line, just as Sam Loyd found with the original puzzle based on a chessboard.

7

Cut out pages 3 to 8 from other side of sheet.
Instructions for making the minibook are on the inside of the back cover.

Follow the Stars: A Hexagonal Rotating Ring

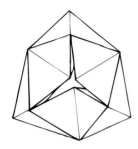

It is interesting to examine this model as it turns and to see the symmetry that it has. You will notice that there are two positions in each rotation where the outline is a regular hexagon. Follow also the colours as the model turns and see how the stars announce the dominant colour of the next set of faces.

Because the model has so much symmetry, there is an enormous number of ways that it could be decorated and you might like to make some further models and to experiment further. The net is not difficult to draw and is given below, together with the correct angles. Any convenient size and any suitable card will do.

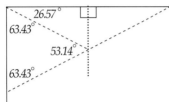

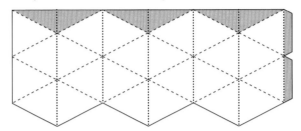

4

Paradoxical Areas

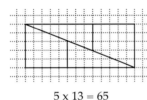

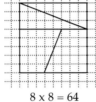

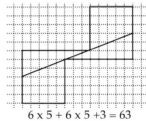

| 5 x 13 = 65 | 8 x 8 = 64 | 6 x 5 + 6 x 5 +3 = 63 |

This curious and well known paradox was first presented by Sam Loyd the elder to The American Chess Congress of 1858. He demonstrated to the amazement of all how an 8 x 8 chessboard could be cut into four pieces and then reassembled to make a 5 x 13 rectangle. Where did the extra unit of area appear from and when it is remade into the square, where did it go to? Some years later, his son, also called Sam Loyd showed how the pieces could be rearranged to give a total of only 63 units.

The secret lies entirely in the distribution of the area and on the tendency of the eye to unconsciously straighten lines which are very nearly straight. Thin slivers of area seem to disappear while squarish blocky areas are given full value. Other ingenious variations on these themes were studied and developed by Harry Langman and Paul Curry. Our model is yet another variation.

6

Shapes of Constant Width

A circle is a curve of constant radius and also a curve of constant width. Its properties allow it to make either a wheel or a roller.

A circular wheel can be fixed to an axle and used to carry loads. The axle passes though the centre of the wheel. The wheel is possibly the greatest invention there has ever been.

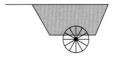

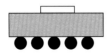

Circular rollers can be used to carry a slab, which is either the load or a platform for the load. As each roller is left behind it must be carried again to the front, but progress is possible even over uneven or relatively soft ground, as the builders of the Pyramids or Stonehenge knew well!

Someone who had never thought seriously about the problem might be forgiven for assuming that a circle is the only shape that has this property. However, as our curious model shows, this is not the case.

8

Score along ◄ - - - - ►
and then cut out pages 9 to 14.
Instructions for making the minibook are on the inside of the back cover.

Shapes of Constant Width

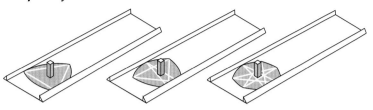

Place each of the rollers within the frame and roll it back and forth, noticing how it always reaches to the top line whichever part of the curve is uppermost.

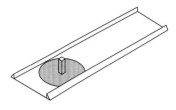

Observe also that only the circle could be used as a wheel because although the others are of constant diameter, they are not of constant radius. As the other shapes roll along the channel, the centre handle does not travel horizontally but moves up and down.

As a further experiment, it is interesting to roll British seven-sided fifty-pence and twenty-pence pieces along inside the frame and to see that they are also shapes of constant width. This property is of vital importance when coins are used in slot machines as they need to roll smoothly down metal channels as they are sorted, weighed and identified.

9

Pop-up Parallel Pyramids

This model made use of two pop-up pyramids which are arranged in an opposed way so that the smaller one disappears inside and becomes invisible just as it becomes parallel to the larger one. It is an amusing example of one of the paper engineering mechanisms that are so much used in pop-up books for young children.

You might like to make a pop-up cuboid which folds flat but which pops up to look much more solid than it really is. The net is given here.

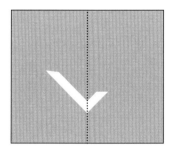 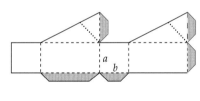 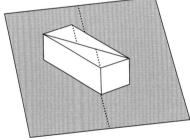

If you make the base the same size as the pop-up pyramids, (about 85mm by 95mm), then values of a = 25mm and b = 50mm gives a good sized cuboid.

11

A Triangular Dissection

This model folds and unfolds in an attractive way and illustrates several important mathematical truths.

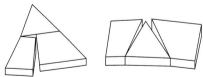

1. It illustrates that the sum of the angles of a triangle is the same as the sum of the angles on a straight line (180°). It also illustrates the properties of corresponding, alternate and interior angles of parallel lines and that the exterior angle of a triangle is equal to the sum of the two interior opposite angles.

2. It shows that the area of a triangle is the same as the area of a rectangle with the same base and half the height. Usually people remember that the area of a triangle is equal to 'half the base times the height'. However, this is of course equivalent to saying 'half the height times the base'.

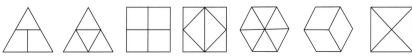

If you would like to experiment with other drawings and designs which dissect, then we suggest that you use regular polygons divided in a regular way. Experiment first on flat card and then make a three-dimensional model when you have discovered something which works well.

13

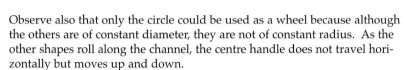

THE
MINIBOOK

Cut out pages 9 to 14 from other side of sheet.
Instructions for making the minibook are on the inside of the back cover.

The Double Helix

This double helix model is reminiscent of the DNA Molecule and is constructed from a linked series of isosceles tetrahedra. Note that all the lines which join one tetrahedron to the next are in parallel planes which are perpendicular to the axis and that each one is rotated relative to its neighbours by 45°. After four tetrahedra the total rotation is 180° and thus the fifth tetrahedron is parallel to the first. The sequence of colours brings out this relationship. To complete one turn and a total of 360° takes 8 turns exactly. In the model, there are ten such tetrahedra, showing how the pattern repeats. In a DNA molecule, the sequence would continue for thousands of turns. Notice how the outer edges form two separate spirals. They have been coloured differently to emphasise this point.

It is interesting to construct another double helix of different rotation. It is not difficult to calculate the angle of the isosceles triangle required. If x is the base angle of the isosceles triangle which makes the net, then the value of x for a given angle of rotation y is given by

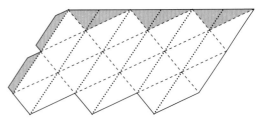

$$Cos\ x = \frac{\sqrt{2}\ Sin\frac{y}{2}}{2}$$

10

For real DNA the value of y is 36°. The chain of tetrahedra can be made as long as you wish.

The Double-sided Magic Square Puzzle

9	6	15	4
16	3	10	5
2	13	8	11
7	12	1	14

In the actual puzzle

Upper side rows
Red, yellow, blue, green

Underside columns
Blue, red, green, yellow

12

This 4 x 4 magic square is an example of a very special kind of magic square called a 'diabolic' magic square. It uses the numbers from 1 to 16 once each and they are arranged in such a way that each row, each column, both diagonals and every 2 x 2 group of four adds up to 34. It can be proved that there are 48 different arrangements of the numbers 1 to 16, not counting simple reflections and rotations. The example given here is one of them and you can use it to see the remarkable number of ways that the numbers sum to 34.

The puzzle makes use of two different examples of diabolic squares, one on the upper side and one on the lower. Neither of them is the example given here and without additional information it would be far too difficult to solve. This additional information is provided in the form of colour coding. All the numbers in the same row on the upper side are the same colour and all blocks in the same column on the underside are the same colour. The orders of the colours however are different! There are lines on the base of the box which show what these colours should be.

Use all this information about the colours and the properties of diabolic magic squares to solve the puzzle. It is a fine example of the need for logical thinking!

Flip-flop Parallelepipeds

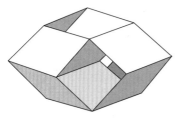
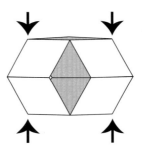
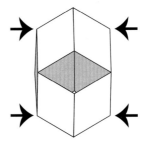

Each of the twelve faces of this shape is a 60° & 120° rhombus and the rhombuses are joined together in a curious way so as to make four connected parallelepipeds which will flip into two different positions, both flat.

Since it is hollow, each side of every face can be seen and so there is nowhere to hide any flaps. The puzzle for us was to find a net so that the 24 rhombuses would glue together back to back and so require no extra flaps. We found it an intriguing and difficult puzzle to solve. Can you find such a solution yourself?

Experiment with rhombuses with different angles, say 30° & 150° or 45° & 135° and see what happens. Do they flip just as well and can you find other interesting properties?

14